eBay Shipping Simplified

How to Store, Package, and Ship the Items You Sell on eBay, Amazon, and Etsy

Table of Contents

Getting Started

Shipping is one of the most frustrating areas for online sellers (even if you've been doing this for a while). The good news is: it doesn't have to be.

That's what this book is all about.

It's a short, easy to understand guide that will help you get over your shipping phobias and help you pack and ship your items like a pro.

When you're done reading this book, you'll have a better understanding of –

- How to store items after you post them for sale, so they are both easy to find and safe from possible damage.

- What your shipping options are. We'll cover shipping with the United States Postal Service (USPS), Federal Express (Fed Ex), common carriers, and home pick up.

- What services you need to use to comply with seller requirements. Examples of this are delivery confirmation, signature delivery, and different tracking options.

- How to use eBay and PayPal shipping solutions to print your labels. We'll also explore third party shipping solutions such as Stamps.com and Endicia, and why you may want to use them.

- Finally, we'll dig into international shipping. You'll learn about eBay's requirements to sell internationally, how to fill out customs forms, how to set customer delivery expectations, and how to simplify international shipping.

You should be able to read this short guide in less than two hours, and immediately be able to use the information you learn to ship smarter, quicker, and less expensively.

Before we continue, I want to take a moment to introduce myself and help you understand why I'm the guy to help you with your shipping needs for your online business.

Why listen to me?

Hey there, Nick Vulich here.

If you're like me, I'm sure you're probably a little skeptical about taking advice from someone without knowing a little bit about them first.

I've been selling on eBay since 1999. Most of my online customers know me as history-bytes, although I've also operated as its old news, back door video, and sports card one.

I've sold 30,004 items for a total of $411,755.44 over the past fifteen years, and that's just on my history-bytes id. Right now, I've cut way back on eBay selling to focus on my writing, but I still keep my hat in the game. That way I can stay current with the challenges my readers face every day when they go to sell on eBay.

I've been an eBay Power Seller or Top Rated Seller for most of the past fifteen years, which means I've met eBay's sales and customer satisfaction goals.

This is the eighth book I have written about selling on eBay. The first two, *Freaking Idiots Guide to Selling on eBay*, and *eBay Unleashed*, are aimed more towards how to get started selling on eBay. *eBay 2014* is directed at more advanced sellers and tackles many of the challenges top rated sellers face in the eBay marketplace. *eBay Subject Matter Expert* suggests a different approach to selling on eBay – building a platform where customers recognize you as an expert in your niche, and buy from you because of your knowledge in that field. *Sell It Online* gives a brief overview of selling on eBay, Amazon, Etsy, and Fiver. *How to Make Money Selling Old Books & Magazines on eBay* talks specifically about what I know best, how to sell books and periodicals on eBay. *eBay Bookkeeping Made Easy* helps sellers understand how to keep track of the money they are earning, and how to take advantage of the tax code to make even more money.

eBay *2015* is an attempt to tie it all together. For those of you who've been following along and reading all of my books, some of this is going to be a rehash. The section on bookkeeping is taken directly from my book *eBay Bookkeeping Made Easy*. It's not the entire book, but enough to give you a good primer on what it's going to take to run an eBay business. Some of the materials in the sections on shipping and international selling come from my book *eBay Shipping Simplified*. Again, it's info you need to know and apply today to thrive on eBay.

My goal is to help you become as successful as you wish to be.

Ship Like A Pro

Understanding how to send the items you sell is just as important as knowing which items to sell.

Online sellers are going to face two different types of shipping situations: domestic (shipping within your home country) and international (shipping outside of your home country). Many sellers spend years trying their hardest to avoid making international sales because they're afraid of the extra paperwork involved or that there may be excessive damage claims, theft, or negative feedback caused by shipping or communication glitches.

The truth is international shipping isn't any more complicated than domestic shipping. It's just a matter of learning and getting used to the extra paperwork involved.

Domestic Shipping

Most of the shipping you're going to do is considered domestic shipping, or shipping within your home country.

The first thing you need to understand is the Post Office offers several different ways to ship items. The shipping method you choose depends upon the item you are shipping, its size, value, and how quickly you want it to arrive.

Here is a breakdown of the most common shipping services available from the post office, and the different items you can ship with them.

- **Media mail** is designed to send books, CDs, DVDs, and other educational materials. Media mail does have a few restrictions. The material cannot contain any advertising pages, so most magazines are ineligible for media mail shipping.

  Packages sent by media mail are subject to inspection by the Post Office, so if you do include inappropriate items, they can send the items back to you—postage due. The main advantage to sellers from using media mail is it's cheaper to ship heavier items like books. Because of this, you can offer your customers a less expensive delivery option. This is especially important if you are selling in the book category because eBay requires sellers to provide an option priced at $4.00 or less.

Delivery time is usually 3 to 8 business days but can vary based on the season. At Christmas time, it can take as much as two to three weeks to deliver a media mail package so be sure to give buyers a heads up – "Hey. It's cheap, but it's slow." That way they understand it's the post office, not you.

- **First Class**. If you're shipping smaller items (less than 13 oz.) first class is going to be the most economical method available. You can ship just about anything—books, clothes, DVDs, CD's, jewelry, stamps, postcards, you name it. The problem is tracking is not available on all first-class packages, so you cannot offer proof of delivery.

  If you're mailing flat items like baseball cards and postcards, then you cannot add tracking. Your package is required to be a minimum of 1/8" thick. Delivery time is usually 1 to 3 days depending on where you are sending your package.

- **Priority Mail**. Most items sold by online sellers, ship by priority mail. It has several advantages over other services including:
  1) You can send heavier items than first class,
  2) Most items arrive within 1 to 3 days, and
  3) Tracking is available for all packages, so you have proof of delivery for eBay and your customers, and

4) The Post Office provides free shipping materials, so you don't have to invest in boxes and other expensive packaging materials.
5) You can schedule a pickup, and the post office will send a carrier to your home or business to pick up your packages.

The disadvantage to using priority mail is that it is more expensive than first class or media mail.

- **Priority Mail Flat Rate** takes the guess work out of shipping. You can ship whatever will fit in the package regardless of the weight anywhere in the United States for a preset fee. Flat rate a great option for buyers and sellers because it's less expensive to ship heavier items or multiple items that will fit into a single package.

  Like regular priority mail—it's quick, offering 1 to 3-day delivery, comes with delivery confirmation, and packaging materials are free from the Post Office. Be sure you use the Flat Rate Priority Mail boxes when using this service.

- **Standard Post** is a less expensive option for mailing parcels and oversize packages. The usual delivery time is 2 to 8 business days. Tracking is included in your shipping fees.

- **Express Mail** offers overnight delivery service to most areas in the United States. If your customer needs an item quick, this is the service for them. Be aware it's expensive, and the fees depend on the size and weight of the package you are sending.

Like Priority Mail, Express Mail offers free packaging materials and delivery confirmation. Sellers also receive $100 of insurance free with most parcels sent, and signature delivery confirmation which eBay and PayPal require on more expensive packages.

- **Priority Mail Express Flat Rate** offers next day delivery (in most areas), plus the added convenience of easier to understand rates. When you use the flat rate boxes anything you mail (regardless of weight) ships for one fee, so if you're shipping heavy items—this is the service for you.

If you want to get more information on these delivery services check out the following link. https://www.usps.com/ship/compare-domestic-services.htm

Package Your Items Like a Pro

How you package the items you sell makes a significant difference in how buyers view you as a seller.

If you just toss your items into a box or envelope, it's going to leave a sour taste in the minds of your buyers. Their purchases are likely to arrive damaged or with bumped and scuffed up packaging that looks like it's been run through the ringer.

I know many books recommend recycling used boxes, packing materials, and such to use for your shipping. In my mind—that's the worst mistake you can make.

You only get one chance to make a good first impression. If your package arrives all scuffed up, or with all sorts of squiggly lines where you crossed out previous addresses, customers are going to be concerned about their purchases. If that's the way you package stuff, your buyers are going to think "God help me" about the stuff you put inside the box.

Set Up Your Shipping Station

Most sellers I've worked with ship their items from the same desk they use to list their items. If you're a part-time seller, that's okay. If you eBay for a living, I'd recommend a separate shipping station.

Here's why.

Shipping is a specialized task. To do it right you need a lot of space and all of your packaging materials and supplies nearby. I have a separate desk and table set up for shipping. I only use my shipping computer when I ship or track shipments. It's an older castoff, but it serves the purpose. I have two printers hooked up to it...a Zebra LP 2844 and a Samsung laser printer.

Most of my shipping labels get printed on the Zebra. I use the laser printer to print packing slips and thank you cards. I also have a postal scale that attaches to the computer through the USB port. It's digital and can accurately weigh up to twenty-five pounds in one-ounce increments. The weight is automatically transferred into Stamps.com with one click of my mouse, so there's never any guesswork involved. I typically round up to the next ounce to add a little wiggle room for tape or the label.

I have sturdy warehouse shelving set up opposite to my desk. The bottom row has flat boxes in various sizes. The next shelf has priority mail boxes and envelopes. The shelf above that has stay flat mailers and padded mailers. The top shelf has all my miscellaneous supplies—shipping labels, paper, extra rolls of tape, box cutters, and Sharpie markers.

Everything is nearby. Once I get started, I can typically package and ship thirty or forty items in an hour. Before I had my shipping station, it always took twice as long because I was running from here to there looking for stuff, or trying to find a good spot to spread all my stuff out.

Storage Solutions – Make Your Items Easy to Find

Hands down, the best thing I ever did for my eBay business was to devise a storage system that both protected my items from being damaged, and made them easy to locate when it came time to ship them.

The storage system you need will depend on what you sell and how many items you have for sale. Keep in mind; your business is going to grow over time. If you have a hundred items for sale today, odds are you'll have a thousand things by the end of the year, and ten thousand within five years. I know from experience—no matter how much room you think you need for product storage triple it, and odds are—you'll still be short of space.

Most of what I sell is lightweight flat material— magazines, magazine articles, prints, and vintage advertisements. Individually none of these items take up a lot of space. The thing is I've got over 25,000 of them, along with close to 1,000 antique books so taken together my inventory consumes a massive amount of space.

When I first started selling, I only had a few hundred items, so I set everything out in piles. When I sold something, I had to sort through countless piles of stuff to find it. It took some time, but it worked.

Fast forward six months. I had over twenty-five hundred items listed for sale online and the longest part of my day was spent trying to locate all the items that I sold and needed to mail.

That's when it hit me—I needed an inventory management system.

I bought some one-inch circular labels at Walmart and started marking my items beginning with one. The number I gave each product was my item stock keeping unit (SKU).

Every item gets a new SKU#. That SKU # controls the object as it moves through the listing, storage, and sales process. When I'm ready to scan pictures for the item listing the images are saved with that SKU #. When I list them on eBay or Amazon, I note the SKU # in the product description. That makes it easy for me to locate the item when it sells. I just need to open the product listing, make a quick note of the SKU # and go to that location to retrieve the item.

It's a slick system, and it makes it easier for someone else to step into my shoes and keep shipping items should I be sick or if something happens to me.

....

Like I said, most of my items are flat, and roughly 8" x 12" in size. I store each article inside of an archival insert sheet. There are two stickers on the outside of each insert sheet. One contains the SKU #. The other is a 1" x 3" label that contains the reference information—the magazine the article or print appeared in, and the month and date of publication.

Because everything is a uniform size, I was lucky enough to discover a magazine collector's box is the perfect storage unit for my items. Each box holds roughly 350 items. All in all, I've got about 25,000 items, so that works out to about seventy boxes.

I picked up some storage shelving and ran it along the side walls of one area in my basement. I have seventy boxes. Each section of shelving holds twelve boxes, so that's six sections of shelving.

When I shopped for shelving, I wanted something lightweight and easy to move around, yet strong enough to hold everything. I settled on heavy-duty polyurethane shelving rated at 200-pounds capacity per shelf. It stands five-foot high times three-foot wide, so the shelving for my base inventory takes up an eighteen-foot space. But, I've still got the books. They take up about the same amount of space along the opposite wall.

That's my inventory solution. Everything is up on shelving off of the floor. All the articles I have for sale are tagged with a numerical SKU # that makes them easy to retrieve when I sell them.

Your solution may be entirely different than mine. You need to base it on the type of items you sell, how much inventory you have, and the space you have available for storage.

The best advice I can give you is to sit down and really give your situation some thought. Think about where your business is now, where you want it to be a few years down the road, and what other products you're likely to carry in the future.

Over time the most likely change you're going to encounter is the need for more space.

Must Have Supplies

There are certain equipment and supplies you need to keep on hand so you can ship smart.

>> Packaging material. Make sure to stock up on boxes, padded mailers, stay flat mailers, bubble wrap, and tape. The worst thing that can happen is to be in the middle of packaging up your orders, and then discover you don't have the supplies you need.

If you ship priority or express mail stop by the post office and pick up the supplies you need. Better yet, hop online and check out https://store.usps.com/store/browse/category.jsp?categoryId=shipping-supplies. Order your boxes ten, twenty-five, or more at a time depending upon how quick you go through them. The post office will deliver them free within two to three days.

If you need to purchase boxes, padded mailers, or stay flat mailers—consider Uline - http://www.uline.com/. They have decent prices and quick delivery.

Wal-Mart carries a great selection of boxes in their shipping supply aisle. The prices are good, especially when you compare them to the big box office supply stores.

I've also had good luck buying supplies from several suppliers on eBay.

. Value Mailers

http://stores.ebay.com/VALUEMAILERS?_trksid=p2047675.l256
3

. Royal Mailers

http://stores.ebay.com/Royalmailers?_trksid=p2047675.l2563

>> **Postal scale**. If you sell online, you need a postal scale. I know a lot of sellers try to fudge it and just guess at weights. Trust me. No one is that good. Every ounce you guess wrong costs you at least seventeen cents. Over the course of a year you could easily save a hundred dollars or more.

Best advice: buy a good digital scale. You can find scales with weight capacities starting at five pounds. I recommend choosing one from USPS.com. They have a good selection, and they hold up well.

>> **Printer**. The printer you use is a matter of preference. I like to use a Zebra label printer because it prints a small compact label you can peel off and stick on your package. There's no messing with tape, or ink cartridges because it's a thermal printer. The next best choice is a laser printer. The ink is less expensive, and it prints quicker. There's nothing more aggravating than waiting for a slow ink jet printer to finish printing your label. The last choice is an ink jet printer. It's slow, but it will get the job done. If you use adhesive-backed labels an ink jet printer is your best bet. Whenever I tried them in my laser printer, they were too thick and jammed it up. ·

>> **Shipping tape**. I usually pick up my tape at Sam's Club or Wal-Mart. You can buy single rolls or save a few bucks and buy them in six packs. My only recommendation is not to buy the cheapest

tape you can find. It tears, it splits, and it's a mess restarting the roll.

>> **Bubble wrap**. If you're packaging china, old books, or other fragile items you're going to need bubble wrap. Here's one item it's okay to reuse. Good places to purchase bubble wrap are Sam's Club, Wal-Mart, or online.

>> **Box cutter**. Be sure to keep a couple of box cutters and plenty of extra razor blades on hand. You want to package your items right, and the best way to do that is to give everything a snug tight fit. To do that you need a box cutter with a sharp blade so you can easily refit boxes.

>> **Peanuts** are those little white foam half circles shippers use to line their packages. They're all static filled and stick to everything. I hate them and refuse to buy anything else from sellers that use them. Use peanuts at your own risk; they're a sticky mess.

Packaging Tips

Okay. You've set up your shipping station and stocked up on supplies. Now it's time for *Packaging 101*.

The best tip I can give you is always to choose the right type of packaging, and err on the side of more packing materials, not less. Don't skimp on packing material.

Tip #1. Choose the right type of packaging. If you're shipping a newer book or a paperback, it's okay to use a padded mailer. If you're sending a rare book or vintage book, you need to package it differently. Use a box and make sure you wrap it inside a sealed plastic bag, and then wrap it with newspaper or bubble wrap. It keeps the corners from getting scuffed or bent, and it protects the book from moisture damage should your box be exposed to water.

If you're shipping china, glass figurines or other fragile materials pick a box about six inches larger all around than what you are shipping. Line the box with bubble wrap or wadded up newspapers. Next, wrap each item in bubble wrap or newspaper and tape it up, so it is secure. Lay the item in the box and cover it with bubble wrap or newspaper. Continue doing this until the box is full. Build another layer of bubble wrap or wadded up newspapers at the top. You'll know you've got it right when you shake the box. If you feel stuff shifting around, open the box and add more packing material.

When you ship electronics, laptops, or tablets, your best bet is to send them in the original box. If that isn't possible, find a box just slightly larger than the item you're going to ship. Build a nest in the box using foam, bubble wrap, or wadded up newspapers. Place your item in a sealed plastic bag, to prevent moisture damage. Wrap it several times with bubble wrap. Place the item in the box. Wrap any accessories, discs, power cord, etc. separately and put them in the box. Build a nest around the top of the box before you seal it to ensure the item can't be shaken in transit. Tape all of the way around the circumference of the box, length wise and width wise. Doing this ensures that the tape won't break free where the box can come open in shipment.

If you're shipping clothes, you can pop a shirt or t-shirt into a priority mail bag. If you're ship jackets, jeans or multiple items use a flat rate priority mail box to reduce your costs. If you're unsure which is cheaper—regular priority mail or flat rate, weigh it out and let the numbers do the talking.

I'm not going to describe any more scenarios, just understand that you need to adapt every packing situation to the item you are shipping.

I've received close to a thousand packages over the last fifteen years. Some of them were perfectly packed, some were adequate, and quite a few arrived banged up and had the items I purchased hanging half way out of the box or missing.

Tip #2. The best time to decide how to pack an item for shipment is before you list it.

Think about it. If you sell a computer or rare figurine—how are you going to determine shipping charges if you don't know how you're going to pack and ship it?

In my case, I have hundreds of rare newspapers dating from 1806 to the Civil War period, but I don't have a cost-effective way to ship an individual paper to buyers. If I fold the paper to make the size manageable, I will ruin a good part of the items collectability. To ship a single paper would require me to buy an oversized casing for it, and then a custom box to put it in. Packaging could easily run forty to fifty dollars before shipping costs. That's a hefty chunk of change to add to a paper I'm selling for twenty-five dollars.

The economics don't work out in this case, so the papers remain in my private collection for now.

Make sure you're not going to go underwater on the items you sell. Before you list an item, determine what it's going to take to ship it. What kind of packaging materials do you need? How much is shipping likely to cost? Is the item expensive enough to require insurance? If so, how much is that going to cost?

Know what you're looking at up front because after the sale you can't come back and ask the customer for more money.

A lot of sellers box their items up at the time they list them. They weigh the package, input the weight into the eBay shipping calculator. If, and when, the item sells they grab the box, print a label and drop it in the mail.

I say to do whatever works for you.

Just keep in mind buyers always have questions. You may need to open the box up to answer a question or to shoot a quick picture or two. Also, not every item sells. You may need to bundle that item up with several other items to make a sale.

Do I Need to Offer Free Shipping?

Free shipping is the biggest bugaboo facing online sellers right now.

eBay encourages sellers to offer free shipping, and they promote items with free shipping to buyers, because of this many new sellers think they are required to provide free shipping. Let me assure you: that's not true.

You don't have to offer free shipping on any of the items you sell. However, you may want to provide free shipping. Here's why?

Typically sales increase when you offer free shipping. There's something about "free" and "shipping" that makes buyers loosen up their purse strings and spend more money. I'm not sure why, but the word "free" is one of those magical keys that can get consumers to pull the trigger and spend more money.

Keep that info tucked away in the back of your head for a moment.

Just because eBay likes free shipping and consumers like free shipping doesn't mean it's the magical ingredient you've been searching for to increase your sales and profits. It needs to be the right combination that's good for both of you. That means you need to be able to make a profit, and your customer needs to get a good value when you offer free shipping.

How does that work?

If you're selling lightweight, easy to ship items free shipping should be a no brainer. Let me repeat that. If you're selling light items, you can send in an envelope or padded mailer and ship for under a dollar you are probably better off giving your customer free shipping rather than trying to charge them that buck. So, if you're selling postcards, baseball cards, small knickknacks, and inexpensive jewelry items that you mail in a regular envelope—mark your item up a buck, and give your customer free shipping.

If you're selling heavier items, low margin items, or custom made items free shipping may make sense. Before you pull the trigger, do your research. Investigate what other sellers with similar items are doing. If everyone else is offering free shipping, you're going to be better off following the pack, unless...and, this is a big unless. If everyone else has marked their item up enough to cover shipping, plus a couple of extra bucks for profit it might make sense to charge shipping and price your item as low as you can while still holding a decent profit.

If most sellers in your category offer free shipping, and some charging for shipping, you may want to test the waters. Offer a few items with free shipping, and a few with your regular shipping charges. Run with the method that makes the most sales for you.

If you're the only one selling a product and you're making a killer profit, go ahead and give your customers free shipping. It's like extra icing on the cake. It's one more reason to buy from you.

Katen Raj wrote one of the better discussions I've read about free shipping on *CPC Strategy Blog*. Give it a look if you need a little extra help working through this issue. http://www.cpcstrategy.com/blog/2012/04/the-free-shipping-formula-for-online-retailers/

Setting Shipping Rates in eBay

Setting shipping rates is another tricky area that can confuse sellers.

Here's the least you need to know.

- If you're a Top-Rated Seller or want to be a Top-Rated Seller you're required to provide tracking information for all your domestic sales. You are also required to post tracking information back into the listing on a minimum of 90% of the items you sell.

- Top-Rated Sellers are required to ship all their items with a one day handling period.

- If the value of any item you sell is over $200, you have an obligation to provide signature delivery confirmation.

If you're not a Top-Rated Seller and don't have any intention of becoming one, it's still a good idea to provide delivery confirmation on every item you send. It protects you from bad buyers who may open an item not received case because they know they will win if you can't provide proof of delivery.

Now we'll get down to the nitty-gritty of setting up shipping in your item listings.

To set your domestic shipping options look for the section labeled *add shipping details* on the sell your item form.

The first choice you need to make is to select your shipping method from the drop-down box. There are four possible options: flat cost, calculated, freight, and no shipping— local pickup. Flat cost is where you charge all buyers the same shipping rate. Calculated shipping uses the eBay shipping calculator to figure shipping based upon your item weight and where you are shipping it. Freight is for larger items too big to ship by the USPS or UPS. Items shipping by freight are carried by a semi or common carrier.

If you sell large items that need to ship by common carrier keep in mind that eBay's freight calculator only works up to 150 pounds. If your item exceeds 150 pounds you need to use flat rate shipping. You also need to understand a few things about truck lines. Most carriers only require their drivers to pull your item to the back of the truck. It's up to your customer to have people available to help them get their item out of the truck and carry it inside the house.

You need to explain this to your customers in your listing description, and again in the shipping instructions you send the buyer after the sale. Here's another tip. You can request the truck line to call your customer the day before delivery. Sometimes they will do it; sometimes they don't, so try not to make too many promises.

To set up calculated shipping click the blue lettering that says *calculate shipping*. This option opens a pop-up box. Fill in the options, and you're ready to go.

If you're using flat rate shipping, click in the box that says standard shipping. Select the shipping service you want to set up, and enter the shipping fee in the smaller box to the right where it says cost. If you want to offer free shipping for a service, put a check mark where it says free shipping. To provide more shipping options click the blue lettering that says *offer additional service*.

To offer local pickup, check the box where it says *Local Pickup*. Be careful when you select this option because local pickup is not available in all categories.

Think long and hard before you offer local pickup for your items. Do you really want to invite customers into your house? Over the years, I've had some local buyers insist on picking up their items to save on shipping. Most times I've delivered the items to their business or met the customer outside of McDonald's or another local business. It's less risky, but a major pain in the backside.

Best advice: avoid local pickup whenever possible.

If you set up flat shipping rules, you can check the box to apply them. If you would like to set up or edit your rules, click on the blue lettering that says *edit rules*. The pop-up box will walk you through setting up shipping discounts. Keep in mind if you modify the top set of rules the changes are only for the listing you are currently working on. If you want to create a discount for all your listings you need to scroll down to the bottom of the pop-up box where it says Promotional Shipping Rule (applies to all items).

If you haven't used this feature, I would suggest giving it a whirl. You'd be surprised at how many buyers will shop for additional items to save a few bucks on shipping.

The next choice you have is to select the *handling time*. If you're a Top-Rated Seller, you are required to ship all items within one day so be sure to choose that option.

The final item gives you a nudge to add next day shipping to your listing. I don't offer the service unless buyers contact me and say they must have next day shipping. My reason for not offering next day shipping is very few people request it, and you have deadlines you need to meet to get the item to the post office on time. It takes more effort than it's worth.

That's it. Your shipping options are set.

Here's another quick tip, so you don't have to go through this with every item you list—set up one of your listings as a template, or when you list new items pull up one of your old listings and select the option to sell a similar item. When you use either of these options, all your previous info transfers over to the new listings. Use the info you want to keep, type over or delete the unwanted info.

Printing Shipping Labels Using eBay & PayPal

Both eBay and PayPal allow sellers to print shipping labels directly from their sites. The process is easy to use and allows you to print professional looking labels and invoices to include with your shipments.

Print eBay Shipping Labels

The easiest way to print shipping labels using eBay is to go into your *Selling Manager*. In the left-hand column find where it says *Selling Manager Pro*. Just down from there you'll see the word *sold*. Select it.

That's going to bring up a list of your sold items. Locate the item you want to ship, and scroll over to the far-right column labeled actions. The first thing you should see is *Print Shipping*.

When you select *Print Shipping,* it takes you to the eBay ship your item page. When you click the page is prepopulated with all your item information.

At the top of the page, it shows the description, the price paid shipping fee, shipping service paid for, and the expected delivery date. The left-hand column contains the shipping information—the buyer's address and your address. If you need to make a change (to either address), select where it says change, and enter the correct shipping information.

Just below the address details, you'll see a box labeled Add message to buyer email. I have a standard thank you message in here, but you can use it to tell your customer a little more about the item or direct them to your store specials. It's up to you.

The center column contains the package details. It's where you choose the carrier, add shipping options, and choose your mailing date. eBay has two approved carriers the United States Postal Service (USPS), and FedEx. My shipping experience has all been with the USPS, so that's what I'm going to cover here. If you ship using FedEx, select them as the carrier and follow the prompts to complete your shipment.

Getting started, the first thing you need to do is select your carrier. In this case, choose USPS.

Use the next box to select your shipping service. The choices are priority mail, first class package, parcel select, media mail, and priority mail express. The priority mail and priority mail express options let you choose the level of service you want.

After you've selected your service, you have the choice of printing the auction number or some other message on the label. Check the box and type in your message. The default message is the auction id.

The final box lets you choose the mailing date. You can choose today, tomorrow, or the next day. The reason for this is you're supposed to mail your package the same day you print the label. If you print the label today but don't send your package for two days, you should change the date. I've never had a problem with the post office if I'm a day or two late dropping the package in the mail, but now you know the correct way to do it.

The third column shows your postage cost broken down by the postage cost, the delivery confirmation fee, and the total cost. Below that, you have an option to hide the shipping so buyers can't see how much actual shipping cost you. It's your choice—if you're playing by the rules and charging actual shipping, let your buyers see the shipping cost. It will prove you're on the up-and-up.

When you're done, click purchase postage. When you do this, your PayPal account is charged the shipping fees. The next screen will show a mockup of the label. You can print a sample, or print the label.

After the tag prints, the program will automatically transfer tracking information into the item listing so buyers can follow the movement of their package throughout the course of shipment.

Alternatively, you can print your postage labels directly from PayPal. To get started open your PayPal account and locate the transaction you want to print the postage for. Click on the text where it says *Print shipping label*. It brings up the same shipping page we used above, so you can follow through using those directions.

Do I Need Insurance?

When eBay allowed sellers to charge customers for insurance, I required all my buyers to purchase it. It saved a lot of hassles. If the item gets lost, insurance saves a lot of hassle and haggling with customers.

What I discovered after shipping over 30,000 items is very few items are lost, stolen, or damaged in transit. I think I've had two damaged packages, and three lost packages in fifteen years. So, is insurance really necessary? It depends on you, and your tolerance for loss. Most of the items I ship cost between twenty to twenty-five dollars. Insurance fees cost close to two bucks for each package. Take two bucks times thirty thousand shipments, and that's close to sixty thousand dollars.

My losses in all this time have amounted to under one hundred dollars. If I buy insurance for every item, I ship it would cost close to $60,000. When you look at it that way—insurance doesn't make sense.

But...insuring my more expensive packages does make me feel all warm and fuzzy inside. Because of that, I decided to pick a number where I would insure my shipments. If the value exceeds that amount I purchase insurance. For me, the magic number is fifty dollars. For you, it may be ten dollars or one hundred dollars. The best I can tell you is to choose your threshold for loss and insure all shipments that exceed that number—that way you can sleep nights.

Here's the least you need to know about insurance.

- eBay no longer allows sellers to charge buyers for insurance. You can roll it into your shipping costs, or you can bury it in the price of your item.

- Filing an insurance claim with the Post Office is a pain in the rear end. It takes a minimum of thirty days for the post office to reimburse you. Many times, it can take two or three times that long.

- When you sell something on eBay, it's hard to prove the actual value of an item, especially for collectibles and one-of-a-kind items. Just because you paid five bazillion dollars for a rare candy bar wrapper doesn't mean that's the value of your item.

- You may have insurance, but your customer doesn't care about that. They don't want to wait thirty days or more to get their money back. If you make them wait for a refund odds are you're going to receive negative feedback.

With all of that said, how do you file an insurance claim? The easiest way is to do it online. Go to the following link https://www.usps.com/ship/file-domestic-claims.htm. It will walk you through filing an insurance claim for a lost parcel.

Here are a few of the highlights to keep in mind.

You need to upload tracking info for the item, a copy of the sales receipt or your eBay auction listing number (to prove value), your insurance receipt, and if you received a damaged item—you need to save the item, along with all packaging materials until the claim finishes processing.

If for some reason, you can't file the claim online call (800) 275-8777, and they will send a claim form.

Using a Third Party Shipping Provider

eBay's shipping label service is great, but sometimes you need a little more oomph to boost your sales and simplify things even more.

I've been using Stamps.com for nearly ten years, and it's been a great alternative for me. Other people have had good luck using Endicia to handle their shipping needs. Both services charge a monthly service fee for using them.

I know what you're thinking. Wait a minute Nick; I'm trying to save money, not spend even more.

Believe me, I understand. The thing is I save a lot of money using Stamps.com to power my eBay shipping. Here's why I use it, and how it saves me money.

What got me hooked on Stamps.com is it's the only way I can ship my items first class international without going to the post office and having them print labels for me. If you use eBay's shipping solution or Click-N-Ship® you can only ship internationally using priority or express mail. When I do that, international sales go down because of the extra shipping costs involved. The extra sales I get by offering the less expensive shipping solution more than cover the $15.99 monthly fee.

One of the other reason I like using Stamps.com is it collects information from all of the platforms I sell on and lets me handle all of my shipping from one central location. For me, that means I can ship the items I sell on eBay, Amazon, bid Start, and my own website all from the same program console.

3 of screen

I don't have to jump from site to site to ship everything. If I need to look up shipping info for an item—it's all in Stamps.com.

It's convenient. I like that. It's worth the extra fifteen dollars a month it costs me to use the service.

To get started with Stamps.com click on the following link http://www.stamps.com/. Select get started to register for a new account. Most times they offer a sign up special that gives you a free postal scale, $25.00 in free shipping credits, and miscellaneous other goodies, along with a one-month free trial.

Once you're ready to go, you can connect all your seller accounts.

What I'm going to do next is give you a quick walkthrough on how to connect your merchant accounts, and how to print postage using Stamps.com. (I assume Endicia works similar to this but I've never used that service so I can't provide you with specifics.)

Don't worry. I'll make this quick and painless.

Setup Shipping Accounts

There are two ways to set up your accounts. Select *Manage Sources* in the toolbar at the top of the screen, or select *batch* from the toolbar in the left-hand column.

Choose Create Profile, and select the data source you want to create.

Printing Postage

When you open your Stamp.com dashboard, there is a command bar running across the top of the screen. There are four main tabs that you'll use over and over again: import orders, manage sources, print, and add order.

- Import orders lets you collect your orders from all of the sites you sell on and bring them into Stamps.com.

- Manages sources allows you to add, delete, or edit data streams.

- Add order allows you to print a label for a package where the customer is not included in any of your data streams. An example is when I send out a review copy of one of my books. The recipient is not in my data stream, so I need to set up a one-time shipment.

- Print pulls up the screen to print your shipping label.

Okay, let's assume you just sat down at your desk and you're ready to start shipping. What do you do?

Select <import orders> from the top menu bar; you'll be prompted several times about actions that are in progress. Most often Stamps.com wants permission to update addresses to match the official address in the postal system computer. Click okay.

After a little while, all your orders will appear in a spreadsheet in the middle of the screen. Select the item you want to mail, and click on the recipient name. The shipping screen for that customer.

Off to the left-hand side of the screen, you will see your name and address. Below that, you will find your client's name and address. You can make whatever changes you need to the shipping address here. The next line is labeled email address. Check the box in front of it, and it will populate with your customer's email address. When you check this, it will send shipping and tracking info to your buyer. The box right after this is cost code. You can make an internal note here if you are tracking categories for shipping.

The next column contains your shipping options.

If you have a USB scale, it will transfer the weight with the click of a button. I usually round up to the next ounce or two depending on the item I'm shipping. That gives me a little wiggle room for the label and tape.

After this, you need to choose the type of mail piece— package, thick envelope, etc.

Then you select the mail class –

- First Class
- Priority Mail
- Express Mail
- Parcel Post
- Media Mail

Place a check mark on the tab to select the mail class. When you do this, it will show the cost for that service. Some classes get blanked out if you can't choose them to ship that particular item. As an example, packages over thirteen ounces cannot be sent by first class so that shipping method would not be available for you to select.

After this, you choose tracking options—delivery confirmation (free with most shipping methods), signature confirmation (an additional $2.35), or none (tracking is not available on flats sent by first class).

Just below this, there is a line labeled options where you can add—certified, USPS insurance, registered, or COD delivery.

The next option lets you select insurance. You can select none or Stamps.com. Your final choice is whether you want to hide the postage cost so buyers cannot see it. If you marked your shipping up a lot, make sure you choose this option.

After you've selected all of your options, click <save> at the bottom of the box. When you do this, a green circle should appear in front of the <order id> on the spreadsheet. To print your postage, choose <print> from the menu bar at the top of the screen. You should see a pop-up that shows the printer name and details. Select <print> at the bottom of the screen to print your label.

International Shipping with Stamps.com

Setting up an order for international delivery is very similar to shipping a domestic order. The only difference is you need to complete a customs form.

Here what you need to do to fill out the online customs form.

Click on the customs form, and it will display a pop-up box for you to fill out. At the top of the form, it asks for a phone number. If your customer listed a number with eBay it will prepopulate. If they didn't give their number, I just fill in 999-999-9999. Otherwise, it will not let you continue.

Where it asks for contents, you have several options. Choose <merchandise>. In the box next to this type a short description. I usually type article or print.

About midway down the page, there is a section labeled *itemized package contents*. The first box asks for the quantity or number of items you are shipping. After that, it asks for a short description of what you are shipping. It should prepopulate from your eBay item description. If the description is too long, you need to shorten it, or the form will not process correctly. The next thing it asks you for is the weight of just the item (without the packaging).

When you've completed all the items, the box at the end of this line asks *add item*. Check that box, and it will move your description into the box below that line.

At the bottom of the pop-up box is a form you need to check. It begins with "I acknowledge..." Once you select the check box, the pop-up box disappears, and you can print your item like normal.

eBay Global Shipping Program

Several years ago, eBay introduced their Global Shipping Program. It's an easy way for sellers to jump into international selling without having to worry about shipping rules, customs forms, etc.

If you've been itching to get started with international sales, but were afraid of the extra work involved I suggest giving it a shot using eBay's Global Shipping Program.

Many small sellers are terrified of international shipping. They've heard so many horror stories about sales that have gone wrong, they're scared to give it a shot. They don't want to fill out customs forms or worry about whether their package is going to make it all the way to Timbuktu or not.

eBay has eliminated all that grief for sellers who use their Global Shipping Program. Sellers list their items just like they normally would. When the item sells, they ship it to an eBay shipping center in the United States.

Bing Badda Boom! As soon as it arrives at the shipping center, your responsibility for the shipment is over. From that point on eBay and their shipping partners assume any liability for getting your package to its destination.

Here's how it works.

When you list your item for sale on eBay check the box to include your item in the Global Shipping Program, and you're ready to go.

Some categories don't qualify for inclusion in the Global Shipping Program. When you bump into these, eBay will flag the item and let you know. I do a lot of selling in the collectibles category. Collectibles manufactured before 1899 don't qualify, so I see this issue pop up quite often. The only way around it is to ship the item internationally yourself. I'll discuss this option in more detail later.

When an item sells using the Global Shipping Program sellers can't send the buyer an invoice. eBay takes care of all this for you. The reason is you have no way of knowing what their shipping fee will be.

Once the customer pays, you will receive your payment notice along with the shipping address. A simple way to recognize a payment made through the Global Shipping Program is the address will include a long reference number.

Ship your item like you normally would. Include delivery confirmation so you can be sure the item arrives at the shipping center. Once you have confirmation the item was received, your part in the transaction is complete.

eBay's shipping partner—Pitney Bowes—will readdress the package, fill out all the appropriate customs forms, and ensure delivery to the customer.

That's the way it should happen. Now and then things don't work out as planned—the customer doesn't receive the item, or it arrives damaged. As a seller, you're supposed to be protected from receiving negative feedback in such a situation. That's right to a point. You need to keep an eye on your feedback profile and keep after eBay to update it should any errors occur.

I received a negative feedback due to a customer not receiving their item. I knew it wasn't received because that's what the seller wrote in his feedback. So, I called eBay customer service and explained the problem. After about fifteen minutes of researching the problem, the rep agreed I was not responsible. He removed the negative feedback while we were still on the phone.

If you experience a similar problem, contact eBay customer service immediately. When you call, have the listing item number and the feedback information available and ready to share with them. Make it easy for eBay to help you.

Overall the Global Shipping Program is an excellent way to increase your sales. At my peak selling period, international sales accounted for roughly thirty-five to forty percent of my eBay sales and profits.

If you're looking for a simple method to grow your sales opt into the Global Shipping Program and give it a shot.

Enable Items for International Shipping

We've already talked about eBay's Global Shipping Program and how easy it is to use, so why would anybody want to ship international packages on their own?

That's a great question.

It comes down to having more control over your shipping options, and the ability to make more sales. When you use eBay's Global Shipping Program, they figure in custom's fees, a markup to pay themselves and their shipping partner an additional profit, plus actual shipping costs. The final number eBay shows your customer for shipping can be mind-boggling and can cost you the sale.

Let me use the products I sell as an example. When I ship items internationally on my own, I charge $5.00 to ship items to Canada, and $9.00 for shipping anywhere else in the world. Sometimes I make a few extra bucks, at times I lose a few bucks, but over time it averages out. Keep in mind; the buyer is still on the line for duty and customs fees when their item arrives.

When I sell the same item using eBay's Global Shipping Program they charge my customer in the low twenty dollar range for Canada, and in the low thirty dollar range for Europe and the rest of the world. My items typically sell for sixteen to twenty-five dollars, so customers are confronted with some serious sticker shock when they see eBay's shipping price.

Self-preservation is one of the primary reasons I ship most international packages myself.

What I'm going to do now is walk you through setting up the international portion of your eBay sell your item form. It's structured very similar to how you set up your domestic shipping options so it should be easy to follow along and use.

....

Everything you need to set your international shipping options can be found in the box labeled *International Shipping*.

The first choice you see is to opt into the Global Shipping Program. In this case, you want to leave that box unchecked.

Below this, you have a drop-down box that offers you the option to select flat rate, calculated shipping, or no additional options. As a quick review, flat rate shipping is where you have one set shipping fee for all buyers. Calculated shipping uses the eBay shipping calculator to determine the shipping price based on the shipping destination. The difference is—flat rate shipping is easier to set up and use, but calculated shipping can give buyers closer to you a break in shipping costs thus giving you the opportunity to grab additional sales from price conscious consumers.

After you choose your shipping method, you'll see another drop down box that says shipping. It gives you three choices: worldwide, chose a custom location, or Canada. I set up a separate price for worldwide and Canada—anymore is overkill in my book. However, if you ship a lot of packages to Mexico, the UK or wherever go ahead and set up a special price for them too. The drop down box next to this lets you choose the type of service you wish to offer, and the box to the right of that allows you to set your shipping price.

Below this, you see a line labeled *offer additional service*. You can use this to provide shipping to an additional location or to provide a different delivery method.

In the *additional ship to locations* you can check off areas you are willing to send to, and the buyer can contact you for more details. Some sellers have lots of rules about where they will and will not ship too. A lot of sellers, mark Malaysia, Italy, Mexico, Russia, etc. off limits because it's all over the internet that other people have experienced problems when they ship packages there. In my book that's all talk. I've sent items to all those countries and never had a problem. All I'm saying is if you're going to put areas off limits or discourage buyers from some areas wait until you have an issue with the area, then evaluate the situation and determine how you want to handle it.

The final line—combined shipping discounts, lets you apply your discount rules to this purchase if you set them up. My items are light and only add a few ounces to the package, therefore, I ship all additional items for free. It's a great way to encourage buyers to continue shopping with you. If you can't offer to send all other items for free—consider offering some type of discounted shipping for additional purchases. It will bring you more business over the long haul.

That's it. You're open for international business. Sit back and wait for the orders to roll in.

I'm going to make one additional suggestion here. Take a few moments to help set buyer expectations. International buyers are like domestic purchasers—they want to purchase their items today and receive them yesterday.

Most times shipping goes smoothly, and items arrive on time, but there are circumstances beyond your control, especially when you're dealing with international customers.

I generally post the following information in each of my listings and include it again in my shipping emails.

"Normal international delivery time is eight to fifteen business days, but it can take as many as four to six weeks—depending on customs and other shipping issues. Please be patient, and take this into consideration when placing your orders."

It helps to set buyer expectations before customers place an order. That way if the client asks where their item is you can refer them back to the info posted in your listing. By giving realistic delivery time frames up front, you're going to save yourself a lot of grief and wasted emails trying to explain why customers haven't received their packages yet.

Remember—International customers have you over the barrel. Tracking is virtually nonexistent for international shipments. The post office is experimenting with international delivery confirmation to select countries, but the service is spotty at best. There's no guarantee the mailman in Canada or the UK will scan your package when he drops it off. He may be having a bad day, or he may be trying to outrun a dog. If your customer decides to file an item not received case you're going to lose because there's no way to provide proof of delivery.

Sorry to be the one to break it to you, but it's a fact of life when you're doing business on eBay. I've only had this happen once. A buyer in Germany opened an item not received case two days after paying for his item. There was no possible way it could travel from Iowa to Germany in two days.

Guess what? It didn't matter. eBay and PayPal decided the case against me because I didn't have proof of delivery. Like I said this happened one time out of five thousand international shipments, so it's not a big deal.

One other quick comment here—many sellers assume proof of shipping is enough to win an international case. It's not. A stamped customs form from your post office is of no help to you if the buyer files an item not received case. If you can't prove the customer received your package, you don't have a leg to stand on.

Customs Forms

The easiest way to handle customs forms is by using online shipping tools. When you use the online tools available through eBay, Click-N-Ship, Endicia, or Stamps.com, they automatically walk you through the forms and ensure you fill them out correctly.

For those of you who insist on doing it old style here's a quick tutorial on customs forms.

The post office uses two customs forms—form 2976 and form 2976-A. Form 2976 is required on all international packages weighing less than four pounds. Form 2976-A is required for all international packages weighing more than four pounds.

Form 2976

LC86075488₉US

Form 2976

The critical information needed for each form is —

- Sender's address
- Recipient address
- Value of each item enclosed
- Total value of all items attached
- Description of contents
- Sender's signature

You have several choices to describe the contents including gift, document, commercial sample, other. You need to check other, and then describe the contents in the description box.

Often sellers will ask you to lie about the value or check the gift box, so they don't have to pay duty fees (taxes). Be aware that if you are caught doing this, it is a felony—subject to fines and jail time. If you're tempted to fudge the form for them, ask yourself—is the sale worth the penalties you could face?

That's pretty much all there is to it.

Have the post office walk you through your first customs form. After doing it once or twice, you'll be a pro and wonder why you ever worried about international shipping.

Form 2976 A

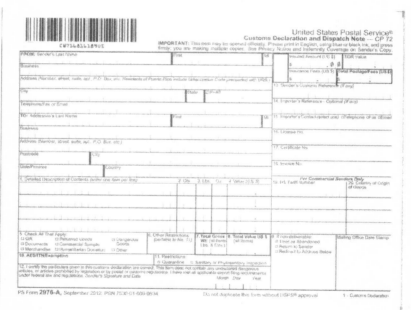

Form 2976A

Remember form 2976 A is for international packages that weigh over four pounds or contain contents valued at over $400.

The essential information needed to fill out form 2976 A is —

- Sender's address
- Recipient address
- Value of each item enclosed
- Total value of contents
- Description of contents
- Sender's signature

You have several choices to describe the contents including gift, document, commercial sample, other. You need to check other, and then describe the contents in the description box.

Special Section for Amazon Sellers

Much of the information I already gave you applies at least in part to Amazon sellers, too. Here's a little more info just for you to help with your shipping solutions.

Amazon has several rules sellers need to comply with when completing a sale and shipping their orders.

1. Sellers are required to ship orders within two days of purchase.

2. Amazon suggests that you include a packing slip with all shipments. Click the *Print Packing Slip* button to the right of the order to print your packing slip.

3. Sellers are not required to have delivery confirmation for their shipments, but Amazon does recommend it.

4. After your item is shipped, return to the order page and click on the confirm order button. When you do this Amazon transfers payment for the item into your account.

5. If you don't confirm the shipment within thirty days of making the sale, Amazon will cancel the order. Even if you shipped the item, you won't be paid for it if you did not confirm shipping in the proper period.

To view, your orders go to Amazon Seller Central. You will see your taskbar at the top of the page. It has four options— inventory, orders, reports, and performance. Click on order to show your current orders. The default view is the last seven days. You can change this by selecting a different period from the drop-down menu.

When you process your postage on Amazon, print a packing slip first. Then choose the button labeled Buy Shipping. It will walk you through printing your postage. When you use this option, it confirms that your item is shipped and Amazon will transfer your payment to your seller account.

If you have any questions here is some info direct from Amazon.

- Ship Orders to Buyers
  http://www.amazon.com/gp/help/customer/display.htm
  l?nodeId=1161252

- Shipping Carrier Contacts
  http://www.amazon.com/gp/help/customer/display.htm
  l?nodeId=201117350

Special Section for Etsy Sellers

Much of the information already gave you applies at least in part to Etsy sellers, too. Here's a little more info just for you to help with your shipping solutions.

Like eBay and Amazon, Etsy lets you print shipping labels directly from your Etsy shop. (This option is currently available only to shop owners in the United States and Canada.) When you're looking at your orders, you'll see shipping options to the right of each item. One button lets you print the shipping label; the button next to it allows you to mark your item shipped.

When you click the print shipping label button, it will bring up the various transportation options available. Click on the shipping type you want to use and follow the directions provided.

If you need more information on Etsy Shipping policies or the shipping tool here are four excellent articles from the Etsy blog.

- 4 Steps to Shipping Success
  https://blog.etsy.com/en/2013/4-steps-to-shipping-success/

- How Do I Use USPS Shipping Labels on Etsy
  https://www.etsy.com/help/article/3107

- Shipping Labels Policy
  https://www.etsy.com/help/article/4646

- 4 Shipping Tips to Customer Satisfaction
  https://blog.etsy.com/en/2014/4-shipping-tips-to-boost-customer-satisfaction/

Bonus Excerpt - 25 Tips & Tricks to Boost Your Sales

(Here's an excerpt from my book, **eBay Ninja Tips & Tricks**. This section provides 25 tips and tricks any online seller can use to grow your business and increase your profitability.)

Here are some tips to help you sell more, work faster, and make more money. Some are simple ideas you can use from day one, others will make more sense as you scale and grow your eBay business.

1) Set up a basic accounting system from day one. Your eBay life will run a lot smoother if you have a bookkeeping system in place from day one. It doesn't have to be anything sophisticated, just a simple way to record all your sales and expenditures. That way when tax time comes around, you have all the information you need close at hand.

My first bookkeeping system was a simple Excel spreadsheet. I used it to track my purchases, sales, and profits. I printed off all my PayPal receipts and stored them in a three-ring binder.

As time went by I transitioned to *QuickBooks*, and then to *Go Daddy Bookkeeping*. Each of these solutions made the process simpler by automating my everyday accounting tasks.

Take some time now to set-up your accounting system.

2) Automate your feedback. Several apps will let you post feedback as soon as a buyer pays for your items. I use to think it was important to leave all my feedback personally, but when I started selling 700 to 800 items per month leaving feedback became a burden.

3) Use eBay's shipping tools. Shipping can easily become one of the biggest time sucks for eBay sellers. When you use eBay's shipping service, it automatically transfers addresses and other information over to the labels it prints. Most shipping options also offer free or discounted tracking on your packages, plus they transfer the tracking info directly into the listing so that buyers can check the progress of their shipments. As a result, you will get fewer questions to answer about when customers are going to receive their shipment.

4) Use free packing materials from the USPS. If you ship by priority mail, get your boxes and envelopes free from the post office. They will even deliver them to you for free.

5) Stop going to the post office. If you're shipping by priority mail, the post office will pick up your packages. You can schedule delivery by following this link
https://tools.usps.com/go/ScheduleAPickupAction!input.action

6) Take advantage of free listing days. eBay offers free listing promotions every month. Take advantage of as many of them as you can to save on fees.
Do the math before you list, or relist any items.

Sometimes you may need to let your items sit for a week or so while you wait for the next special to roll around.

(Note: 12/01/2016 – eBay has scaled way back on free listing promotions since I first wrote this. Occasionally you can still snag a free listing promotion for 500 or 1000 free auction listings, but they are few and far between compared to what they used to be.)

7) Offer free shipping. If it makes sense, offer free shipping on your items. eBay loves free shipping and will promote your items more often when you offer free shipping.

8) Offer a combined shipping discount. If offering free shipping doesn't work for what you sell, consider offering a combined shipping discount to buyers who purchase more than one item. You'd be surprised how many buyers will pick up another item or two when they can get free or discounted shipping on the additional items.

9) Respond quickly to buyer inquiries. Answer questions as quickly as you can. Potential buyers will lose interest if you make them wait to long for an answer. Unhappy customers will be delighted if you answer quickly, and let them know you're eager to help them solve their problem.

When you respond to customers—be positive. Thank them for writing you, and let them know it is a really-great item. If a potential buyer wants to know something about your item, give them a little more information than they asked expected. Build extra-value into every item you sell.

Suppose a customer asks about the battery life on your iPad. Tell them, "It's a really nice iPad, with hardly any signs of wear. I mainly used it between classes. The only reason I'm getting rid of it is my parents gave me a new iPad Air for my birthday. The battery lasts about ten hours if you're just listening to music or surfing the web."

The extra information may tip the scales and help them decide to buy your item.

If it's a buyer who's unhappy with a recent purchase, let them know you're there to help, and that you understand their frustration. "Thank you for contacting me about your recent purchase. I'm very sorry to hear that you are unhappy with your item. I'll be glad to do whatever I can to make it right for you. Here are a few tips that may help..."

Say thank you often as often as possible. Offer to resolve any problems the buyer may have. If it's a potential customer, and they're on the line about whether the item will work for their intended use, or about the condition, I make sure to mention my 100 percent money back guarantee. That takes all the risk out of purchasing my item.

10) Sell International. eBay has a new Global Shipping Program that makes shipping internationally as easy as shipping in the United States. The way it works is you opt into the program when you list your item. When the item sells, eBay collects shipping, fees, and customs duties from your customer. After your customer pays, eBay provides you with the address to their fulfillment center. As soon as they receive your package, your part in the transaction is complete.

From this point on eBay readdresses the package, and forwards it to your customer. They fill out all the customs forms, choose the right shippers, and complete all the heavy lifting for you.

If you haven't opted into the Global Shipping Program yet, give it a shot. Once I started selling internationally, sales jumped thirty to thirty-five percent.

11) Setup your customer FAQ. Let eBay automatically answer common questions for you when buyers inquire about shipping, payment, combined shipping, item details, and returns. eBay answers these questions by responding with the information you provided when listing your items. If you want to add additional info, you can do that as well.

Follow this link to activate your customer faqs.

http://contact.ebay.com/ws/eBayISAPI.dll?ManageSeller FAQ#

12) Accept returns. Buying online is scary, especially when you are purchasing used items sight unseen. When you offer a money-back guarantee, people feel better about buying from you. Often, just knowing they can return an item, will give buyers that extra nudge they need to purchase from you.

Many sellers are afraid to offer refunds because they feel it is one more way buyers can take advantage of them. I've offered a 100 percent money back guarantee for the past seven years, and have had fewer than 25 returns in all that time.

If you want to make more sales, offer a "no questions asked" refund policy, and see what it does for your sales.

13) Add video to your listings. It's a fact. People love video. If you can find a way to add videos to your listings, sales are going to go up.

It doesn't have to be a major production. Shoot a quick selfie video from your iPhone talking about your listing. If you've got something really cool like a model airplane or remote control car, show someone putting it through its paces.

Keep it simple. Just introduce yourself, and what you like about selling on eBay. It will help build trust in you, which should lead to making more sales.

The best way to add video to your listing is to upload it to YouTube. Use the embed code to paste it into your listing page. Be sure to use the old embed code option. It works best with eBay.

[Come June of 2017, video will no longer be allowed in listings. It is part of eBay's active content ban.]

14) Skip listing upgrades. All they do is put extra money in eBay's pocket. The only one I would suggest is subtitle, and then only when you are selling an expensive item.

What subtitle does is give you an extra eighty characters to help describe your item. Words in your subtitle don't show up in search, but when buyers find your item, it gives extra information that may induce them to click into your listing. Keep in mind, if your item doesn't sell, it's going to cost an extra $1.50 when you relist your item, so be sure to remove the subtitle if you don't want to pay for it again, and again. I don't know how many times I paid the extra fee five or ten times because I forgot all about it.

15) Include tracking information with all your shipments.

Packages get lost. Sometimes buyers say they didn't receive your item when they did. Tracking keeps everybody honest. If buyers don't receive their package, they can open an "item not received case against you."

The first thing eBay does is ask for tracking information. If it shows delivered, you win the case. If you don't have tracking information, eBay will accept the buyer's word that they did not receive your package, and refund the cost of your item plus shipping.

16) Set an insure limit. As a seller, you're responsible until your buyer receives their item. If the buyer doesn't receive the item, or it arrives broken, you are responsible. Set a limit you're comfortable losing. Insure any packages that exceed that amount. One-hundred dollars has always been my limit. If I ship packages valued over one-hundred dollars, I insure them. It limits my losses if something goes wrong.

You also need to keep in mind eBay no longer allows sellers to charge for insurance. You need to roll the cost of insurance into your shipping price, or the price of your item.

17) Sell in a variety of formats. Don't limit yourself to auction, or fixed price listings. Shake things up a bit. Be sure to use best-offer and buy-it-now.

If you have a large quantity of items, try one day, three days, five days, seven day, and ten day auctions. Offer one item at auction. Sell a few more at fixed price. Tell people in your auction listing if they want the item now, you also have it available with a buy-it-now.

You never know until you try.

Some buyers enjoy the thrill of bidding. They want to score a bargain. Other buyers just want to purchase the item they want and be done with it. Make sure you are catering to both types of buyers.

18) Try new things. Don't be afraid to experiment. Try new products. Keep the ones that sell, discard the ones that don't. Doing this will keep your inventory fresh, and assure you a constant stream of new products that keep customers coming back to see "what's next."

19) Keep an eye on your competition. If you want to increase your sales, you need to keep an eye on your competition. Watch what they're selling. Keep an eye on any new product offerings they have. Know when they drop a product line. Keep an eye on their prices. Are they going up? Down? Or are they running a string of specials?

Several years ago, my sales dropped significantly for about two months. Finally, it got to the point I needed to figure out what was going on. After a bit of searching, I discovered one of my competitors was getting ready to close his eBay store. He'd dropped his prices from $20.00 each to $2.00, and then $1.00. I couldn't match his prices. But, I did decide this was an opportunity for me to cherry pick his inventory. Over the next few weeks, I grabbed five hundred items that made me a great profit once he was done selling out.

My suggestion is you should make a list of your top five competitors. Keep close tabs on what they're doing. Take notes. Try some of the things they are doing. Over the long run, it will make you a better seller.

20) Set regular office hours. There's a danger to working at home. Because you have everything there, you can be tempted to keep working at it longer than you should. You know what I mean. I just need to list five more sales. I just received a dozen new emails; I better answer them quick.

And, then, there's the biggest time waster of all constantly checking sales. I admit, I still have a problem with this one.

If you can do it, set a time limit. Tell yourself I'm shutting eBay off at 7:00 so I can spend time with my family. So, I can read a good book. So, I can go jogging.

One of the best things you can do is to find a good work/life balance.

21) Read as many books as you can. To be successful, you need to read. Read about how to sell on eBay. Read about what you sell. The more you know about the product line you sell, the more you are going to sell. Buyers love buying from an expert. The more you know about your product line, the more pertinent information you will be able to put in your listings.

If you shop at garage sales, estate sales, or auctions, you're going to recognize bargains, and you should make more money.

22) Write eBay reviews and guides. Share your knowledge with others. eBay guides and reviews give you the opportunity to position yourself as an expert in what you sell.

Writing them doesn't have to be time consuming.

Do you sell DVD's? Did you watch a new movie? Write a short review telling people what you liked about it. Over time, it's easy to post hundreds of reviews. As reader's stumble across your reviews, many of them will check out your eBay store.

Some may even make a purchase, or two.

Do you sell stamps, coins, or baseball cards?

Millions of collectors visit eBay everyday looking for these items. If you write a few guides about grading, collecting tips, how to get the best deal at auction, etc., potential buyers are going to look at you as an expert. Many of them will check out what you're selling.

Use eBay guides and reviews to grow your business.

23) Fill out your eBay profile. Profiles are new to eBay. Like the old MY World, Profiles lets you share information about yourself with other eBay buyers and sellers.

This feature is eBay's attempt to join the social networking revolution. At the top of your Profile page, you can post your profile picture and behind it a banner. You get a short spot to describe your business, and then it shows your feedback.

Below this eBay shows five items you are selling in a scroll bar that allows sellers to look through your items.

The next section is for collections, another new eBay feature. Collections are a Pinterest like feature that let you build picture collections of items you're selling or other items you like that are selling on eBay.

Below that is a section for followers, and then a larger section that shows your eBay reviews and guides.

My advice is to fill out as much of your eBay Profile as you can. People are more comfortable buying from someone they know—even if they only know you from reading your profile. The more you can show potential buyers you're a real person—the more likely they are to buy from you.

24) End your items often. eBay search favors newly listed items. If you have an eBay store with hundreds or thousands of fixed priced listings, end them often. Instead of using good-till-cancelled, list your items for thirty days. Then relist them—one

at a time. It's a pain in the ass, but it will pay off over the long haul.

A ready supply of newly listed items ensures your items stay fresh.

The advantage to you is your items will rise in search each time you relist them. As a result, you will make more sales.

25) Develop an inventory system. One of my biggest challenges occurred about six months after I started selling on eBay. I moved from listing one hundred items to listing over five thousand items.

It became impossible to find items when the time came to ship them. Some days it took me longer to locate the items I sold than it did to print the shipping labels.

When I sold videos, I kept them in boxes scattered all over the basement. Finally, I decided that's enough! I bought a dozen shelves, labeled them from A to Z, and got everything together. It made life a lot easier and saved me over an hour a day in shipping time.

When boxes of videos came in, I scanned them and put them on the proper shelves.

My advice is to develop a good inventory and storage system from day one. It will make your life easier over the long run.

About the Author

My books offer short easy to read solutions to your e-commerce problems. You can read most of them in under an hour. The information can be used to help you sell more products on eBay and Amazon, services on Fiverr, or eBooks on Amazon and Kindle.

Selling online isn't a mystery. It doesn't even have to be difficult.

It's all about getting started. Many people I've talked with have this crazy fear of putting things up for sale on eBay and

Amazon. Somehow, they get the idea they need to do this or that. They worry they don't know enough about what they're doing to do it right. They wonder what they should sell, and about whether they can even do it or not.

That's where my books come in.

They take you hand in hand and walk you through getting started selling on eBay, Amazon, Etsy, and Fiverr. They show you how to market your Kindle books.

My goal is to get you over the speed bumps so that you can be more successful from the get-go.

What are you waiting for?

Most of my books are available as audiobooks. If you prefer to listen rather than read, be sure to check them out.

April 1st, 2017

Nick Vulich
Davenport, Iowa